Last Minute College Financing Guide

Second Edition

Last Minute College Financing Guide

Second Edition

Marianne Ragins

TSW Publishing
P. O. Box 176
Centreville, Virginia 20122
www.scholarshipworkshop.com
TSW Publishing is a division of The Scholarship Workshop LLC

The *Last Minute College Financing Guide* was written to provide
accurate advice to readers. Neither the author, the publisher, nor
any entity associated with the *Last Minute College Financing Guide*
assume any liability for errors, omissions, or inaccuracies. Any
action you take or do not take as a result of reading the *Last Minute
College Financing Guide* is entirely your responsibility.

ISBN: 978-0-9767660-8-7

Printed in the United States of America

This book is available at special quantity discounts for bulk
purchases for sales promotions, premiums, fundraising, and
educational use. Special versions or book excerpts can also be
created to fit specific needs. For more information, please contact
info@scholarshipworkshop.com or call 703 579-4245. You can also
write: TSW Publishing, P. O. Box 176, Centreville, Virginia
20122.

Dedication

To my mother, my husband, and my little ones—your love, motivation, and presence in my life keep me going.

To Aria and Cameron — your input and suggestions were greatly appreciated.

For Gloria Laverne Solomon, Sammie L. Moore Sr. and Dr. Angela E. Grant
As people who truly got the most from life and helped us to get the most from ours, your sunny smiles, loving hearts and generous ways will be remembered forever by all of your family and friends.

CONTENTS

Introduction

If it is currently the late spring or summer of your high school senior year, you have a treasured acceptance letter in hand or you are already on the campus and you still don't have enough college funding, it is officially the last minute for you. Although it can certainly help your short-term relaxation, procrastination is not a friend to anyone. For the high school senior in search of college funding, especially scholarships, it is your worst enemy. Why? For many scholarships, particularly those for amounts of money totaling more than $5,000, the deadlines occur in the fall or winter of your high school senior year. As a result, when April of your senior year arrives, your opportunities may have started to shrink considerably. If you look at *The Scholarship Monthly Planner* (www.scholarshipworkshop.com), a resource designed to help students access and download scholarship applications, write and prepare application packages, and stay on top of scholarship deadlines; you would see many entries for the months of October, November, December and even January. These entries show when to download scholarship applications and complete other activities for specific scholarships. For these same months, you would also see many entries in red for actual deadline dates to apply for various scholarships.

However, if you look at the months of April, May, June or July in *The Scholarship Monthly Planner*, you would see that the scholarship opportunities diminish considerably in the late spring and summer.

So, if it is the month of June and you are reading this guide, what can you do to still find college financing? Actually, you can pursue quite a few options. And this guide is designed to help you explore them.

State Financial Aid Agencies

To determine if you qualify for state funding, you should visit your state financial aid or state grant agency. The term state financial aid agency applies to government organizations that administer state or federally funded aid. In some states, this may be the Board *or* Department of Education or it may be under a separate Commission on Higher Education, Higher Education Assistance Authority or Postsecondary Education department. Regardless of the name, the agency could be a great source for funding your education. Exploring these agencies may help you to uncover scholarships, grants, and other college funding specifically offered to students in your state. Most importantly, many of these sources could have later or rolling application deadlines.

Please note that some states may qualify you for certain grants based on information submitted in the Free Application for Federal Student Aid (FAFSA). You and your parents should complete this form as soon as possible. The FAFSA can now be completed as early as October 1 of the year prior to beginning college. If you have not completed the FAFSA, you should do so immediately by visiting www.fafsa.ed.gov, completing the form, and having your financial information sent to the school you plan to attend. If you have exhausted all government aid and have received an award from the college or university you plan to attend, but it is still not enough, read on. This guide includes many other options you can explore. It also includes information about appealing a financial aid decision from a college or university. Just make sure you thoroughly research all programs offered through your state. Even though the FAFSA may qualify you for some state aid, a separate application may be required for some programs.

Alabama
Alabama Commission on Higher Education
100 N. Union Street
P.O. Box 302000
Montgomery, AL 36130-2000

Phone: (334) 242-1998
Fax: (334) 242-0268
Website: http://www.ache.state.al.us

Alaska
Alaska Commission on Post-Secondary Education and
  Alaska Student Loan Corporation
PO Box 110505
Juneau, AK 99811-0505
Phone: (907) 465-2962, (800) 441-2962 (Alaska only)
Fax: (907) 465-5316
E-mail: ACPE@alaska.gov
Website: http://acpe.alaska.gov

Arizona
Arizona Commission for Post-Secondary Education
2020 North Central Avenue, Suite 650
Phoenix, AZ 85004-4503
Phone: (602) 258-2435
Fax: (602) 258-2483
Website: https://highered.az.gov/

Arkansas
Arkansas Department of Higher Education
Four Capitol Mall, Room 403-A
Little Rock, AR 72201
Phone: (501) 682-4475
Website: http://www.arkansased.org

California
California Student Aid Commission
P.O. Box 419026
Rancho Cordova, CA 95741-9026
Phone: 1 (888) CA GRANT (224-7268)
Fax: (916) 464-8002
E-mail: custsvcs@csac.ca.gov

Website: http://www.csac.ca.gov

Colorado
Colorado Department of Higher Education
201 East Colfax Avenue, Room 500
Denver, CO 80203
Phone: (303) 866-6600
Fax: (303) 830-0793
Website: http://www.cde.state.co.us/

Connecticut
CT Office of Higher Education
450 Columbus Boulevard, Suite 510
Hartford, CT 06103-1841
Phone: (860) 947-1800
Fax: (860) 947-1310
Website: http://www.ctohe.org

Delaware
DE Higher Education Office
The Townsend Building
401 Federal Street, Suite 2
Dover, DE 19901
Phone: (302) 735-4120, (800) 292-7935
Fax: (302) 739-5894
Website: https://www.doe.k12.de.us/ (see Supports < Higher Ed)
or https://www.doe.k12.de.us/domain/226

District of Columbia
DC Office of the State Superintendent of Education
1050 1st Street, NE
Washington, DC 20002
Phone: (202) 727-6436
Website: https://osse.dc.gov/

Florida
Florida Department of Education
Office of Student Financial Assistance

325 West Gaines Street, Suite 1314
Tallahassee, Florida 32399–0400
Phone: (888) 827-2004
Website: http://www.floridastudentfinancialaid.org

Georgia
Georgia Student Finance Commission
State Loans and Grants Division
2082 East Exchange Place, Suite 200
Tucker, GA 30084
Phone: (800) 505-GSFC (4732
Fax: (770) 724-9089
Website: http://www.gsfc.org

Hawaii
Hawaii State Board of Education
P. O. Box 2360
Honolulu, HI 96804
Phone: (808) 586-3334
Fax: (808) 586-3433
Website: http://boe.hawaii.gov/
E-mail: BOE_Hawaii@notes.k12.hi.us

Idaho
Idaho State Board of Education
650 West State St.
P.O. Box 83720
Boise, ID 83720-0037
Phone: (208) 334-2270
Fax: (208) 334-2632
Website: http://www.boardofed.idaho.gov
E-mail: board@osbe.idaho.gov

Illinois
Illinois Student Assistance Commission
1755 Lake Cook Road
Deerfield, IL 60015-5209
Phone: (800) 899-4722
Fax: (847) 831-8549
Website: http://www.isac.org

Indiana

Indiana Commission for Higher Education
Division of Student Financial Aid
101 West Ohio Street, Suite 300
Indianapolis, IN 46204
Phone: (317) 464-4400 or Toll-Free: 1-888-528-4719
E-mail: awards@che.in.gov
Website: http://www.in.gov/ssaci

Iowa
Iowa College Student Aid Commission
430 E. Grand Avenue, 3rd Floor
Des Moines, IA 50309
Phone: (515) 725-3400 or (877) 272-4456
Fax: (515) 725-3401
Website: http://www.iowacollegeaid.gov

Kansas
Kansas Board of Regents
Student Financial Assistance
1000 SW Jackson St, Suite 520
Topeka, KS 66612-1368
Phone: (785) 430-4255 or (785) 430-4256
Fax: (785) 430-4233
Website: http://www.kansasregents.org

Kentucky
Kentucky Higher Education Assistance Authority
Student Aid Programs
P.O. Box 798
Frankfort, Kentucky 40602-0798
Phone: (800) 928-8926
Website: https://www.kheaa.com

Louisiana
LA Office of Student Financial Assistance
P.O. Box 91202
Baton Rouge, LA 70821-9202
Phone: (800) 259-5626
Fax: (225) 208-1496
Email: custserv@la.gov
Website: http://www.osfa.la.gov

Maine
Finance Authority of Maine
Maine Education Assistance Division
P. O. Box 949
5 Community Drive
Augusta, ME 04332-0949
Phone: (800) 228-3734
Fax: (207) 623-0095
E-mail: education@famemaine.com
Website: http://www.famemaine.com

Maryland
Maryland Higher Education Commission
6 North Liberty Street, Ground Suite
Baltimore, Maryland 21201
Phone: (410) 767-3300 or Toll-Free: 1 (800)974-0203
Fax: (410) 332-0250
Email: osfamail.mhec@maryland.gov
Website: http://www.mhec.state.md.us

Massachusetts
The Massachusetts Office of Student Financial Assistance
75 Pleasant Street
Malden, Massachusetts 02148
Phone: (617) 391-6070
Fax: (617) 391-6085
Email: osfa@osfa.mass.edu
Website: http://www.mass.edu/osfa/

Michigan
MI Student Aid
Student Scholarships and Grants
P.O. Box 30462
Lansing, MI 48909-7962
Phone: 1 (888) 447-2687
Website: http://www.michigan.gov/mistudentaid
Email: mistudentaid@michigan.gov

Minnesota
Minnesota Office of Higher Education
1450 Energy Park Drive, Suite 350
Saint Paul, MN 55108-5227

Phone: (651) 642-0567 or Toll-Free: 1 (800) 657-3866
Fax: (651) 642-0675
Website: http://www.ohe.state.mn.us

Mississippi
Board of Trustees
Mississippi Institutions of Higher Learning
3825 Ridgewood Road
Jackson, MS 39211-6453
Phone: (601) 432-6997, in state only: (800) 327-2980
E-mail: sfa@ihl.state.ms.us
Website: http://www.mississippi.edu

Missouri
MO Department of Higher Education
205 Jefferson Street
P.O. Box 1469
Jefferson City, MO 65102-1469
Phone: (573) 751-2361 or Toll-Free: (800) 473-6757
Fax: (573) 751-6635
E-mail: info@dhe.mo.gov
Website: https://dhe.mo.gov/

Montana
Montana Office of the Commissioner of Higher
  Education
560 N. Park, 4th Floor
P.O. Box 203201
Helena, MT 59620-9124
Phone: (406) 449-6570
Fax: (406) 449-9171
Website: http://www.mus.edu/che

Nebraska
NE Coordinating Commission for
  Postsecondary Education
140 N. Eighth Street, Suite 300
P.O. Box 95005
Lincoln. NE 68509-5005
Phone: (402) 471-2847
Website: https://ccpe.nebraska.gov/

Nevada
Nevada Department of Education, Financial Aid
700 East 5th Street
Carson City, NV 89701
Phone: (775) 687-9200
Fax: (775) 687-9101
Website: http://www.doe.nv.gov

New Hampshire
New Hampshire Department of Education
101 Pleasant Street
Concord. NH 03301-3494
Phone: (603) 271-3494
Fax: (603) 271-1953
Website: https://www.education.nh.gov/

New Jersey
New Jersey Higher Education Student Assistance Authority
P. O. Box 540
Trenton, NJ 08625
Phone: (609) 584-4480, (800) 792-8670
Website: http://www.hesaa.org

New Mexico
New Mexico Higher Education Department
2044 Galisteo Street, Suite 4
Santa Fe, NM 87505-2100
Phone: (505) 476-8400
Website: http://hed.state.nm.us

New York
New York State Higher Education Services Corporation
99 Washington Avenue
Albany, NY 12255
Phone: (518) 473-1574, (888) 697-4372
Website: http://www.hesc.ny.gov

North Carolina
NC State Education Assistance Authority
P.O. Box 14103
Research Triangle Park, NC 27709
Phone: (919) 549-8614

Fax: (919) 549-8481
E-mail: information@ncseaa.edu
Website: http://www.ncseaa.edu

> College Foundation of North Carolina
> P.O. Box 41966
> Raleigh, NC 27629-1966
> Phone: (866) 866-2362
> Website: https://www.cfnc.org

North Dakota
ND University System
10th Floor, State Capitol
600 East Boulevard Avenue, Dept 215
Bismarck, ND 58505-0230
Phone: (701) 328-2960
Fax: (701) 328-2961
E-mail: ndus.office@ndus.edu
Website: http://www.ndus.edu

Ohio
Ohio Department of Education
25 South Front Street
Columbus, OH 43215
Phone: (614) 466-6000
Fax: (614) 466-5866
E-mail: hotline@highered.ohio.gov
Website: https://www.ohiohighered.org

Oklahoma
Oklahoma State Regents for Higher Education
655 Research Parkway, Suite 200
Oklahoma City, OK 73104
Phone: (405) 225-9100
E-mail: communicationsdepartment@osrhe.edu
Website: http://www.okhighered.org

Oregon
Oregon Higher Education Coordinating Commission
Office of Student Access & Completion
1500 Valley River Drive, Suite 100
Eugene, OR 97401
Phone: (541) 687-7400
Fax: (541) 687-7414

Website: http://oregonstudentaid.gov

Pennsylvania
Pennsylvania Higher Education Assistance
  Agency (PHEAA)
P.O. Box 8157
Harrisburg, PA 17105-8157
Phone: (800) 692-7392
Fax: (717) 720-3786
Website: http://www.pheaa.org

Rhode Island
Rhode Island Office of the Postsecondary Commissioner
560 Jefferson Boulevard, Suite 100
Warwick, RI 02886
Phone: (401) 736-1100
Fax: (401) 732-3541
Website: https://www.riopc.edu/

South Carolina
SC Higher Education Tuition Grants Commission
115 Atrium Way, Suite 102
Columbia, SC 29223
Phone: (803) 896-1120
E-mail: info@sctuitiongrants.org
Website: http://www.sctuitiongrants.com

South Dakota
South Dakota Board of Regents
306 East Capitol Ave
Suite 200
Pierre, SD 57501-2545
Phone: (605) 773-3455
Fax: (605) 773-5320
E-mail: info@sdbor.edu
Website: http://www.sdbor.edu

Tennessee
TN Higher Education Commission
404 James Robertson Parkway, Suite 1900
Nashville, TN 37243-0820
Phone: (615) 741-3605

Website: https://www.tn.gov/thec

Texas
TX Higher Education Coordinating Board
P.O. Box 12788
Austin, TX 78711-2788
Phone: (512) 427-6101
Website: http://www.thecb.state.tx.us

Utah
Utah Higher Education Assistance Authority
60 South 400 West
Salt Lake City, UT 84101
Phone: (801) 321-7294, (877) 336-7378
Fax: (801) 366-8431
Website: http://www.uheaa.org

Vermont
VT Student Assistance Corporation
Champlain Mill
P.O. Box 2000
Winooski, VT 05404-2601
Phone: (802) 655-4050
Fax: (802) 654-3765
E-mail: info@vsac.org
Website: http://www.vsac.org

Virginia
State Council of Higher Education for Virginia
James Monroe Building, Tenth Floor
101 N. Fourteenth Street
Richmond, VA 23219
Phone: (804) 225-2600
Fax: (804) 225-2604
Website: http://www.schev.edu

Washington
WA Student Achievement Council
P. O. Box 43430
917 Lakeridge Way, SW
Olympia, WA 98504-3430
Phone: (360) 753-7800

E-mail: info@wsac.wa.gov
Website: http://www.wsac.wa.gov

West Virginia
West Virginia Higher Education Policy Commission
1018 Kanawha Boulevard East, Suite 700
Charleston, WV 25301
Phone: (304) 558-2101
Fax: (304) 558-1011
Website: http://www.wvhepc.edu/

Wisconsin
Higher Educational Aids Board
Post Office Box 7885
Madison, WI 53707-7885
Phone: (608) 267-2206
Fax: (608) 267-2808
E-mail: HEABmail@wi.gov
Website: http://www.heab.state.wi.us

Wyoming
Wyoming State Department of Education
122 W. 25th Street, Suite E200
Cheyenne, WY 82002
Phone: (307) 777-7675
Fax: 307-777-6234
Website: https://edu.wyoming.gov/

Understanding Federal Financial Aid

Government assistance comes in a variety of forms. For instance, you can obtain grants and loans from the United States government. Or you can get help from the government as a taxpayer with certain tax credits for educational expenses. The Lifetime Learning Credit and the American Opportunity tax credit are two credits of this type that are explained later in the chapter. State governments also participate heavily in contributing to the students of their states by offering various types of aid programs ranging from tuition waivers to full scholarships.

For federal and some state assistance you will need to complete the Free Application for Federal Student Aid (FAFSA). The FAFSA will help most colleges and universities to determine your financial aid package. The financial aid package usually contains some type of federal aid such as the Pell Grant, work-study, or a Direct or Plus Loan, in addition to university scholarships. For some institutions, you will also need to complete the CSS–Financial Aid PROFILE (College Scholarship Service–Financial Aid PROFILE). You may also have to submit another financial aid form specific to the institution you are planning to attend to determine your aid package.

For information about the CSS PROFILE, visit www.collegeboard.org. To get more information about the federal financial aid forms, visit the following web sites and social media platforms:

Federal Student Aid and Free Application for Federal Student Aid (FAFSA)

Website: http://www.fafsa.ed.gov or www.fafsa4caster.ed.gov

Facebook:
https://www.facebook.com/FederalStudentAid
Twitter: @FAFSA
YouTube:
http://www.youtube.com/user/federalStudentAid

The Student Guide

Website: https://studentaid.ed.gov/sa/ or
http://studentaid.ed.gov/resources#funding
Facebook:
https://www.facebook.com/FederalStudentAid
Twitter: @FAFSA
YouTube:
http://www.youtube.com/user/federalStudentAid

IRS Tax Information and Benefits for Students

Website: http://www.irs.gov/Individuals/Students

Now let's answer a few basic questions that will help you understand the financial aid process and how it works.

What is a Financial Aid Package?

A financial aid package is the total amount of financial aid a student receives. For example, a package could consist of loans, grants, work-study (work-study is a job arranged for you on the college campus and funded by the federal government as part of your financial aid package to assist with college expenses), and scholarships. The contents of a financial aid package are usually communicated to a student in a financial aid award letter or an electronic communication. An example award letter is shown later in this chapter.

How is a Financial Aid Package Determined?

A financial aid package is determined primarily by the FAFSA, and/or the CSS-Financial Aid PROFILE and the financial aid committee/director at the universities or colleges to which you have applied. Both the FAFSA and the CSS-Financial Aid PROFILE are financial aid forms with several differences that help to determine a student's total need. The FAFSA uses federal methodology to determine your need and the CSS-PROFILE uses institutional methodology and may be requested by some private colleges and universities.

What is My Financial Need?

The amount of financial need you have will be based on how much you and your parents can contribute to the total cost of your education at the college you have chosen. The amount you and your parents can contribute plus the amount of outside aid you will receive (such as scholarships that are not from the university or college to which you are applying) is subtracted from the total cost of college attendance to obtain your total need. Your contributions will be based on your current income, assets, etc. To get an estimate of your need and expected family contribution, and for an idea of how much federal financial aid you may be able to receive, visit the federal student aid information web sites provided to you at the beginning of the chapter.

Once need has been demonstrated and is sent to the college on your student aid report (SAR), the institution will determine your total financial aid package and the amount of your need they can meet. Some colleges and universities meet 100% of your need. Some don't even come close. It depends on the institution and the circumstances. You should also keep in mind that if you have been awarded a financial aid award package by a specific college or university and you win an additional merit based non-need scholarship award, your financial aid package at the school may be reduced. It may be reduced because the additional award lowers your total need amount. For example, if your financial aid package at a school is for $15,000 per year and you win a scholarship for $5,000 a year, your award package at the school may be reduced to $10,000 per year. If you win a need-based award, but have already received a financial aid package from a college or university meeting your total financial need you may be ineligible to receive this award even after you've won it, since the award amount can never be higher than your actual need. Some schools will allow you to use the additional monies towards books and personal expenses. When applying to schools, ask about their policies regarding this issue. Also some scholarship programs will work with you on this as well. So if you've won a scholarship and you think you may not be able to use it, contact the scholarship program to let them know. They may be able to suggest additional options.

Now, let's explore the primary way your need and financial aid package is calculated—the financial aid forms.

The Financial Aid Forms

There are two primary financial forms accepted by colleges and universities. The most common application accepted and requested is the FAFSA (Free Application for Federal Student Aid). If you are applying for any government aid, such as the Pell Grant or a SEOG grant, you will need to complete the FAFSA. This is one of your first steps in securing aid for college. Even if you are applying for merit-based scholarships many colleges and universities will require you to either complete the FAFSA or the College Scholarship Service–Financial Aid PROFILE. There is a fee for the using the CSS–Financial Aid PROFILE. You can get information about obtaining the FAFSA from your high school guidance office, from public libraries, or directly from the U.S. Department of Education. Completing the FAFSA online is also very easy and streamlined at www.fafsa.ed.gov. It's also free to complete and file. If you have any questions concerning how to obtain the FAFSA, call (800) 433-3243 or (800) 4FED-AID.

To be eligible for federal financial aid you must:

1. Be a U.S. citizen or an eligible noncitizen.
2. Have a valid Social Security Number.
3. Be registered with the Selective Service if you are male and between the ages of 18 and 25.

4. Show financial need, except for some of the loan programs.
5. Have a high school diploma, a GED, pass a test approved by the U.S. Department of Education, meet other standards your state establishes that are approved by the U.S. Department of Education or show that you completed a high school education in a homeschool setting approved under state law.
6. Be enrolled or accepted in an eligible program as a regular student and be working toward a degree or certificate.
7. Be making satisfactory academic progress.
8. Be enrolled at least half-time to be eligible for Direct Loan Program funds.
9. Sign a statement on the Free Application for Federal Student Aid (FAFSA) stating that you are not in default on a federal student loan and do not owe money on a federal student grant and you will use federal student aid only for educational purposes.

The FAFSA will determine your eligibility for the following federal financial aid programs:

- *Pell Grant*—Federal grant given to students who are enrolled full-time or part-time and have financial need;

amount is determined by the depth of the student's need. As long as you attend an eligible school, you do not have a minimum grade point average requirement nor a specific academic requirement. This grant is usually the first form of financial aid a student obtains before getting other types of federal aid and some scholarships. For this reason, many scholarship programs require you to fill out the FAFSA when applying for their scholarship, especially if the scholarship is a need-based rather than a merit-based scholarship. The Pell Grant may be paid directly to you or credited to your student account by your school. Or if your Pell Grant exceeds the balance on your account, the remainder may be distributed directly to you.

- *Federal Supplemental Educational Opportunity Grant (SEOG)*—Given in addition to the Pell, this grant is awarded to students who have extreme financial need. The amount is determined by the institution you attend. Most schools deplete their SEOG funds early, so it is imperative that you complete the FAFSA as soon as possible.
- *Work-Study*—A part-time job at the college or university you attend that

pays you money to offset your educational expenses.

- *Loans* — There are various types of loans available from the federal government. The William D. Ford Federal Direct Loan (Direct Loan) Program is the largest. For loans under this program, the U.S. Department of Education is your lender. Visit www.studentaid.ed.gov for additional information about any of these direct loans. The following information is a brief summary for each type of loan available from the federal government:
  - o Direct Subsidized Loans (*the government pays the interest while you're in school at least half time*) are need based and made to eligible undergraduate students to help cover the costs of higher education at a college or career school. Your school determines the amount you can borrow which cannot exceed your financial need. Visit www.studentaid.ed.gov for current loan limits.
  - o Direct Unsubsidized Loans (*you pay the interest while you're in school or it accrues and is added to the loan balance*) are non-need based loans made to eligible undergraduate, graduate,

and professional students. Your school determines the amount you can borrow. This amount may be based upon the cost of attendance and other financial aid you receive. Visit www.studentaid.ed.gov for current loan limits.

o Direct PLUS Loans are made to parents of dependent undergraduate students and also graduate or professional students to help pay for education expenses not covered by other financial aid. Visit www.studentaid.ed.gov for current loan limits. The limit on a PLUS Loan is equal to your cost of attendance minus any other financial aid you receive. For example, if your cost of attendance is $10,000 and you receive $3,000 in other financial aid, your parents can borrow up to-but no more than $7,000.

o Direct Consolidation Loans can be a combination of all of your eligible federal student loans into a single loan with a single loan servicer.

For more information on the requirements for federal financial aid programs, consult *The Guide to Federal Student Aid* published by the

U.S. Department of Education. Call 1-800-4FED-AID or visit the web site at www.studentaid.ed.gov to obtain it.

To receive financial aid for each year in college, a FAFSA renewal form must be filed. The amount of your financial aid award may change each year. This could happen if the costs at the college or university you are attending increases or if your family's financial situation changes. Changes in your family situation or your situation, if you filed as an independent student, include reduced or increased salary, another child entering college, one of your parents starting college, a long-term illness, or a disability.

Considering a Loan?
Special Note for Parents and Students

Before signing the promissory note for a student or parent loan, please think twice about attending a school that will leave you in significant debt after you graduate. Ponder these questions before you promise to pay:

- Are there alternate schools that can meet your needs?

- If you choose to attend the school that greatly exceeds your current and future budget, have you reviewed the school's job placement statistics for recent and past graduates?
- Have you explored the occupational prospects for the career path the school will start you on?
- Do you know the projected salary levels? For example, if you can get a job when you graduate, will your salary put you at the poverty level once you factor in your student loan payments?

If these figures look promising, at least you've done some homework before incurring debt.

Sample Financial Aid Award Letter

(Many colleges and universities communicate this information in an electronic format rather than as a letter.)

Anytown University
Office of Financial Aid
Aid, Georgia 00001

March 15, 2025

To: Caroline F. Student
        Student ID #
        P.O. Box 4000
        Raleigh, North Carolina 29333

On behalf of the Financial Aid Committee, I am pleased to inform you that your request for financial aid has been approved for the upcoming academic year. Please read carefully the conditions listed below and the appropriate messages on the reverse side of this notice.

Approved:
$8500.00   XYZ Alumni Scholars Scholarship
$5000.00   NYS General Scholarship
$2000.00   Federal College Work Study
$1500.00   Federal Perkins Loan
$17000.00   Total Approved

Lynn Smith
Director of Financial Aid

Please read the following financial aid conditions carefully:

- All grants and loans will be credited directly to the student's account each term in the following manner: 37 ½ % Fall, 25% Spring, 37 ½ % Spring. College work-study eligibility is the amount a student may earn working on campus. The actual amount may depend on the number of hours worked. Students who work under the College work-study program will be paid biweekly.
- Academic scholarships are automatically renewed for students who maintain a cumulative 3.0 grade point average. All other scholarships require a minimum 2.0 for renewal unless otherwise specified.
- All grants, loans and work eligibilities are awarded for one year, and you must reapply every year by completing an Anytown University financial aid application and other required financial aid forms such as the FAFSA. Further information is available in the Financial Aid Office.
- Students are required to report all financial awards received from other sources. The Financial Aid Office will re-evaluate the student's need for assistance and a revision in the award may be necessary.

____ I accept the financial aid award and the conditions listed above.

____ I reject the financial aid award listed above.

Tax Assistance for College Expenses

The government also provides aid in the form of tax credits, which can help ease the burden of college expenses. Some of the major tax credits and deductions are explained in the following:

The American Opportunity Tax Credit

This credit is a per-student, partially refundable tax credit. Eligible students can claim up to $2,500 for expenses on tuition, fees, and educational materials in the first four years of post-secondary education. This credit is dependent upon your filing status and income level. See publication 970 at http://www.irs.gov or your tax professional for additional information. Low-income families who owe no tax may also be eligible to receive a credit refund of up to $1,000 for each qualifying student.

The Lifetime Learning Tax Credit

This tax credit focuses on adults who want to go back to school, change careers, or take a couple of courses to upgrade their skills. It is also applicable for students who are already in college such as juniors, seniors, graduate students and professional degree students.

Using the Lifetime Learning credit, a 20% tax credit can be taken for the first $10,000 of tuition and required fees paid each year. For example, a secretary, whose family has an adjusted gross income of $60,000, wants to attend a graduate program at a public university ($2,700 tuition). Her intention is to upgrade her skills to get a management position eventually. The secretary has been working and out of college for the past 12 years. If she uses the Lifetime Learning credit, her family's income taxes could be cut by as much as $540. The Lifetime Learning tax credit is available for tuition and required fees minus grants, scholarships, and other tax-free educational assistance. See publication 970 available at www.irs.gov or your tax professional for additional information.

Coverdell Education Savings Accounts
If you have a child under age 18, you can deposit $2,000 per year into a Coverdell Education Savings Account in their name. Earnings in the Coverdell Education Savings Account will accumulate tax-free. If you withdraw the money in the Coverdell Education Savings Account to pay for post-secondary tuition and required fees (less grants, scholarships, and other tax-free

educational assistance), books, equipment, and eligible room and board expenses, no taxes will be due. Once your child reaches age 30, his or her Coverdell Education Savings Account must be closed or transferred to a younger member of the family.

Your ability as a taxpayer to contribute to a Coverdell Education Savings Account may be phased out based on your income level and filing status. See www.irs.gov (publication 970) or your tax professional for additional information.

Early Withdrawals from IRA's
Generally when you withdraw money from an IRA before your reach age 59 ½ you are subject to an additional 10% tax on the money withdrawn. However, if you use the money withdrawn to pay the qualified higher education expenses of you, your spouse, or a dependent in that year, you will not owe the additional 10% tax. See www.irs.gov (publication 970) or your tax professional for additional information.

Tax Free Interest for Education Savings Bonds and Employer Provided Educational Assistance

Normally, interest earned on savings bonds and money provided by your employer to pay for your higher education is taxable. However, the interest earned on certain types of bonds that are cashed in and used for the qualified higher education expenses is not taxable. Your ability to take advantage of this deduction will depend upon your income level and marital status. Likewise, your employer can provide you with up to $5,250 each year for higher education without including this amount in your taxable income. See www.irs.gov (publication 970) or your tax professional for additional information.

Qualified Tuition Plans (QTP) or 529 Plans
Qualified tuition plans can be either college savings accounts or prepaid tuition programs, established and maintained by your state or an eligible educational institution. These plans are frequently called 529 Savings Plans and 529 Prepaid Tuition Plans. The 529 Savings Plan allows your money to grow tax-free for future educational costs and can be withdrawn tax-free when used for qualified higher education expenses. In contrast, 529 Prepaid Tuition Plans allow you to buy tuition credits or certificates for your son or daughter. Then when they are ready to attend college, the

credits or certificates can be used as a waiver or as payment of college tuition. Consult your tax professional or financial advisor for more information.

Lowering the Overall Cost of Your Student Loan

If you are currently repaying student loans, you may be able to take a deduction for interest paid on your student loans. The deduction is available even if you do not itemize other deductions. The maximum deduction is $2,500. It is phased out for certain income levels. See www.irs.gov (publication 970) or your tax professional for additional information. The deduction is available for all loans taken to pay tuition or other qualified higher education expenses.

For additional information about other tax assistance or deductions, please visit the IRS web site at www.irs.gov and read or download IRS Publication 970. You can also call 1-800-4FED-AID.

Going Beyond State and Federal Funding

After you've explored your state and federal aid funding options, you should begin focusing heavily on the local search. Local organizations often have later deadlines than national or more well-known organizations. Wondering how to find them? Contact the following:

- Counselors (high school)
- Career center directors
- Community foundations
- Libraries
- Local associations

You can also conduct an advanced search in a general Internet search engine such as Google or Yahoo! to find community foundations, libraries, or associations in your city. For example, if you lived in the city of Arlington, Virginia, you might include the information in the advanced search section similar to the information in the image below to find a community foundation. Conducting this advanced search uncovered the Arlington Community Foundation. The Arlington Community Foundation as well as other community foundations throughout the country often have information and applications for scholarships available to students in specific communities.

Advanced Search		
Find Results	all of these words	Arlington
	the exact phrase	community foundation
	with at least one of these words	Virginia
	any of these words	

There are community foundations throughout the United States. There may be one in your community too! So make sure to conduct an advanced search to find one available to you in your area.

Using this same type of advanced search method with Google, Yahoo! or another search engine, you should also search for scholarships specifically in your city. For example, instead of "community foundation" for the exact phrase, enter "scholarship" or "scholarships". With this strategy I have found thousands and often times, millions of scholarships listed for specific cities when the results were returned in the search engines. You can even go further by narrowing your search to "music scholarships," or "nursing scholarships".

Or, in addition to city and state, you could search based on your county. Focusing your search in this manner can help you narrow your search to little known scholarships that may have much later deadlines than national scholarships and may even have less competition.

Also check the Internet for the web site of your county school system or school board. Some county systems maintain databases containing local as well as national scholarships that are available to students in the county. The least they may have is an Adobe PDF file you can access. Or they may have a fully searchable database that can be explored based on criteria you input. You can find these databases by asking your counselor, performing an advanced Internet search, or going directly to your school web site (which you should always check anyway).

You can also find last minute funding by contacting all of the following to find scholarships and awards with deadlines you can still meet:

- *Local clubs, organizations, sororities, fraternities, and service clubs*—If you perform an advanced Internet search, you may find some of these organizations and links to scholarship opportunities. However to be thorough (since some may not have a web site), you should use your local telephone book (or www.yellowpages.com) to find a number to call and inquire if the organization has any scholarships or awards available to students in the area. For example, organizations such as these might have scholarship

opportunities or contests you can
enter to obtain college funding:

- Elks Club
- Kiwanis Club
- Masons
- Rotary Club
- Lions Club
- Knights of Columbus
- National Exchange Clubs
- Daughters of the
  American Revolution
- Boy Scouts/Girl Scouts
- Jaycees
- American Legion
- Soroptimist Club
- Optimist Club

- *Companies and banks* — You should
  contact the human resources
  department for all companies and banks
  headquartered in your area. Some may
  offer scholarships that are designed to
  specifically target students in the
  community or general area.
- *Radio and television stations* — Although
  your local radio and television station
  may not sponsor a scholarship, they
  may have had a recent or past guest

who can provide information about local scholarship programs. When calling, ask for the producer who works on educational segments.

- *Parents' employer*—Some employers have corresponding foundations that administer scholarship programs for the children of their employees.
- *Unions*—Ask your parents if they belong to a union and also about how to contact the union to determine if they have a scholarship program.
- *Credit unions*—Credit unions in your area may also sponsor scholarships for their student members.
- Any organization where you or your parents have a membership (i.e. church or faith based organizations)

Last Minute Internet Search Strategies

F or a complete scholarship search on the Internet, start by using all of these services. This is very important since some search engines include scholarships that others may not.

Scholarship Search Engines

College Board Scholarship Search

http://apps.collegeboard.com/cbsearch_ss/welcome
.jsp or
https://bigfuture.collegeboard.org/scholarship-
search

Sallie Mae – Find Scholarships for College

https://www.salliemae.com/college-planning/college-scholarships or www.salliemae.com (search Scholarships)

Fastweb

http://www.fastweb.com
Facebook: https://www.facebook.com/PayingForSchool
Twitter: @PayingForSchool

CollegeNET

http://www.collegenet.com/mach25
Twitter: @CollegeNET

Scholarships.com

http://www.scholarships.com
Facebook:
https://www.facebook.com/scholarships.com.info
Twitter: @Scholarshipscom

UNCF Scholarship Search

https://scholarships.uncf.org/Program/Search or http://www.uncf.org (see Scholarships section on website)
Twitter: @uncfscholarship

Unigo

https://www.unigo.com
Facebook: https://www.facebook.com/myunigo

General Search Engines

Visit Yahoo!, DuckDuck Go, Bing, and Google. Search for terms such as, "college scholarships," "financial aid," "scholarships," and "fellowships." Each of these search engines will give you a list of web sites and articles where the term you searched for is included. This will lead you to specific scholarship program web sites.

You can also use general search engines to determine if an organization you heard about in the news or elsewhere has a web address. For example, if a news article lists a program called the Elks Most Valuable Student Scholarship, put the entire name into the search box of an engine with quotation marks around it. By doing this, you can go directly to the web site if the search engine finds a link.

Visit your public library web site to search for magazine and newspaper articles on the Internet about scholarships. For example, if you lived in Fairfax County, Virginia you could visit the library on the Internet and use the online databases to search for magazine articles. Many of these articles list scholarship programs. Some magazines with previous articles are *Money*, *Ebony*, and *U.S. News & World Report*. You can also go directly to their web sites and perform a search on past articles. Usually, most publications covering finance also publish articles about college aid.

Or you can conduct a search of articles relating to scholarships and financial aid by using Google News Search (https://news.google.com).You can also use Google Alerts (www.google.com/alerts) to get e-mail alerts for recent articles that have been written about scholarships, college, and financial aid.

Get information about federal and state aid available to you by visiting the following sites.

- **U. S. Department of Education**
  o www.ed.gov
- **Tax Benefits for Education**
  o www.irs.gov (see IRS Publication 970)
- **Resources from the office Federal Student Aid**
  o http://studentaid.ed.gov/resources#funding.

Social Media

Social media can help you find scholarship and award programs, particularly those that have frequent announcements and updates. Use the search fields of social media sites to find scholarships, contests, and prizes open to students. To begin, type "scholarship program" or associated terms into the search box on a social media platform such as Facebook.

You can also do the following to use social media to your advantage:

- If you like certain pages for scholarship and college related programs on Facebook, you may get alerts on scholarship application availability, deadlines, tips, and more.
- Following programs on Twitter might also keep you aware of tips, deadline extensions, application availability, and announcements.
- Viewing YouTube videos can help you understand a program's mission, values, and goals, which can help you prepare for an essay or

interview. Or, in the case of a competition, you may be able to view previous performances or submissions to help you prepare and perfect your own.

Funding Strategies for Those Already On Campus

Are you already enrolled in college and you're trying to find money to continue? If so, then this section is written especially for you.

- Look for scholarships and awards as soon as you know you may need more money. Even if you don't need additional funding, you can apply for merit scholarships, which don't require you to have financial need. Merit scholarships can look great on your résumé or curriculum vitae. Be careful! Some schools may reduce your financial aid package if you win an outside scholarship. If this happens, contact your financial office immediately to discuss your options.

- Review books such as *Winning Scholarships for College* and directories such as *Peterson's Guide to Scholarships, Grants and Prizes* for sources of financial aid.
- Consider entering contests such as writing, photography, and beauty that offer monetary awards.
- Contact the financial aid office at your college or university. Make sure to read your college or university catalog for a list of fellowships, endowments, and scholarships to get an advance idea of money for which you qualify. You should also visit the financial aid section of your school web site. It's best to have a good idea of the school's available student aid funds so you can ask specific and general questions about possible money to help you finish your education.
- Visit web sites such as www.finaid.org, www.fastweb.com, www.scholarshipworkshop.com,

and scholarships.com for information about scholarships and loan repayment programs.

- Speak with your academic department to get information about sources of non-need and need-based funding for students in your major.

- Contact the alumni association for your school in your hometown and ask if they offer scholarships or financial aid to students currently attending the school. Many often do, yet the funds are not heavily advertised.

- If you attend a United Negro College Fund (UNCF) college or university, visit www.uncf.org for information about numerous scholarships that may be available to you.

- Contact professionals who are already working in the field you are planning to enter or obtain your degree. Ask if they are aware of associations or organizations that could help you complete your education. For example, if you're studying in the field of veterinary medicine, contact a veterinarian.

Alternatively, if it's anthropology, contact an anthropologist. Doing so may or may not help you find a scholarship opportunity, but it could get you a paid internship and/or valuable work experience, which can help you win scholarships, grants, or open doors to other opportunities. Since professionals in your local area may know of smaller, community and regionally based organizations that offer support to students, you should do this in addition to trying to find national associations and organizations that may be listed in a book or have a web site.

- If you attend a public college or university out of your home state, check with your financial aid office to determine your eligibility for an out of state tuition waiver. Some states have reciprocity agreements. Get more information about reciprocity in the fifth edition of *Winning Scholarships for College*.
- If you are currently employed either as an intern, co-op, or at an off-campus job, ask your employer if

they have scholarships available for current employees, interns, or co-op students. Many employers have tuition reimbursement programs. And some employers also offer scholarships in addition to paid positions for college students who intern or co-op with them. Even if the company does not fund all or part of the education of an intern, your job experience will enhance your résumé for future employment and scholarship consideration. See the fifth edition of *Winning Scholarships for College* to get more information about how to approach your employer for tuition reimbursement. In addition, some companies make employee scholarship programs available to their employees after a certain time period. For example, if you've worked at Wal-Mart while going to college, you may be able to win one of the scholarships they have set aside for employees.

- Contact church/religious, civic, and community organizations in your hometown and where your school is located. Many will help students by offering additional funds to keep them in school. Some also have scholarship programs for students in or from the area.

- Check with your advisor. They may be aware of funding opportunities that are available to you.
- Try to get work study or on-campus employment in one of your school's on-campus offices.
- Research service scholarships for loan repayment possibilities. If you're willing to work for an organization either during, before, or after you graduate for a specified time period, you may be able to get help with outstanding student loans or current and future college bills. Organizations such as AmeriCorps may have such programs. See the chapter, "Scholarships and Awards for Community Service, Volunteering and Work" in the fifth edition of *Winning Scholarships for College* for more information about these types of programs.

- Talk to professors and other staff members at the college or university you attend. Some may fund small scholarships.
- Contact the athletic office if you participate in any type of sport. Athletic scholarships can be offered for many different athletic activities such as swimming, lacrosse, and tennis. To get a sports scholarship, you don't always have to play football, basketball, or baseball. Refer to the chapter in the fifth edition of *Winning Scholarships for College*, "Scholarships for the Unnoticed Athlete."
- Contact the department for your major course of study to see if they are aware of scholarship opportunities for students in that area of study. Also, contact the department for your minor course of study to see if they are aware of financial aid available to you.
- If you participate and have a serious interest in activities such as music, dance, theatre, or art, contact the directors or departments for these

activities to see if there are scholarships available to you in these areas.

- Review directories that list grants in specific areas to see if there might be aid opportunities that could apply to you. For example, check out *Foundation Grants to Individuals* or *The Foundation Directory* online. Although you may not find specific scholarship programs, you will see organizations that may be receiving grants in order to fund scholarships for students like you. Based on the contact information you find for the organization that received the grant, you can follow-up with them or use the Internet to get the requirements to apply for the scholarship or financial aid program on which the grant was based and awarded. A site such as the Foundation Center at www.fdncenter.org is a good start for finding these resources and other information.

- Contact your local newspaper and the Chamber of Commerce to see if they may be aware of aid opportunities with local businesses in the area.

- Contact national and professional associations and organizations in your area of graduate study. For example, marketing students might contact the American Marketing Association, or architectural students might contact the American Institute of Architects, and so on. To find associations and organizations in your area of study to see if any of them offer scholarships, look at the Encyclopedia of Associations published by Gale Research, which can usually be found at your local library. You can also visit the Internet Public Library (http://www.ipl. org) and go to the Special Collections area to search for "Associations on the Net." Although the Internet Public Library is no longer being updated, it still has a treasure trove of useful information about associations. This section is organized by category.
- Contact community foundations. The Berks County Community

Foundation of Berks County, Pennsylvania offers various scholarship opportunities for residents in the area. So does the Community Foundation of Southern Indiana, (CFSI). To see examples of web sites for communities with these types of foundations, visit www.bccf.org for Berks County and www.cfsouthernindiana.com for the Community Foundation of Southern Indiana.

- Contact honor societies in your area of study—for example, engineering, anthropology, and music. Refer to *College Survival & Success Skills 101* for a comprehensive list of societies and their web addresses.

- Check with organizations that benefit certain groups to which you inherently belong (i.e. legally blind, women, and minority). For example, the American Association of University Women (AAUW) administers a scholarship program for women.

- Check on companies in need of future employees in your area of study or a related area.

Using Crowdfunding for Last Minute Funding

Crowdfunding allows students to tell their story over the Internet to thousands of people quickly and with minimal effort. Individuals all over the world with access to the Internet see a student's words and hopefully become compelled to contribute with funding. There are several popular crowdfunding sites such as www.gofundme.com or www.gogetfunding.com.

Following are some tips for a successful crowdfunding campaign:

- You should have great visuals. If you can take a picture of yourself with something from your future college or university, like a sign or mascot, it might help to encourage alumni and others to donate because it may give them an immediate visual connection with you.

- Use social media. Let others know about your campaign on your social media accounts but ask ALL of your family members with active social media accounts to share. If you attend a church or faith based organization, ask them to share on their social media. Also contact the youth and young adult ministry, scholarship ministry, education ministry and similar ministries to let them know about your campaign.
- Don't forget to create a hashtag specific to your campaign. This can make it easier to follow your campaign and see the interest it's getting.
- Check with your current or future university to see how you can connect with alumni via social media, email, or another way to share your campaign. Also check out the web site and social media accounts for the alumni association in your hometown.

- Give a compelling and interesting name to your campaign. It should be something that people can easily remember. For example, Amy Needs Your Dollars for College - I Could Be Your Future Physician.
- Post updates. Let people know how it's going for you. Share success and failure. And let them know how much you appreciate the money already contributed and how wonderful it will be when you reach your campaign goal. You might also share what you've done with money contributed so far.
- Offer an incentive. You could offer something like a free hour of live or web based tutoring for one student at the local high school or middle school for every $100 or $1000 you receive. Or you could offer to spread the love by helping at a food bank, a shelter or some other community organization one hour per month every time you reach a $1000 threshold (or some other number) in your campaign.
- In your story, share your future career plans and how you plan to help others in the future just like donors will

hopefully help you now. For example, you could discuss setting up a mentoring program or joining an organization such as Big Brothers Big Sisters once you graduate. Or for those with family members affiliated with a Greek organization mention future participation in the community service efforts of those organizations (if you successfully pledge).

- Let donors know exactly how the money will be used. For example: I need $5,000 for my room and board deposit at XYZ university.
- Consider adding a video to your story. Something memorable would be best. People love videos with animals. Maybe include your favorite pet in a video saying how much you will miss him or her doing their favorite stunt while you're away at college. But you're planning for a great future for both of you in your own home after you graduate. Or perhaps the video could be of you showcasing a special skill or talent you plan to share with others as a future college student or graduate.

Crowdfunding is a great way to raise last minute cash for school. However, your funding campaign may not raise as much as you want or need. You should make every effort to explore additional sources of funding explained in other sections of this guide. Also don't forget to explore scholarships, grants and awards for current college students. Don't stop looking for additional funding until all your current and future college bills are fully funded.

Appealing a Financial Aid Decision

If you've been accepted to your dream school and the financial aid you've been offered is not enough for you to attend, what can you or your parent (s) do?

- Once you receive a financial aid award letter from a school you really want to attend, don't be afraid to appeal the decision or ask for a professional judgment review if the aid is not enough. In your appeal make sure to include any extenuating circumstances such as another child or a parent in college, reduced family income, disability, divorce, or excessive consumer debt, which may be affecting your circumstances and your ability to afford the tuition and related costs of attendance. Many schools will reevaluate their decision.

- If you have received scholarships or large amounts of non-need aid from another institution but you have your heart set on another school that has not offered you nearly as much, make sure that the institution you really want to attend is aware of the money the other school offered you. They may match the other offer if they really want you to attend their institution in the upcoming academic year.

Steps for Appealing a Financial Aid Decision or Requesting an Adjustment/Reconsideration

Step 1

Review your financial aid award carefully and consider the following:

- Has anything changed about your financial situation since you completed the financial aid form?
- Is there an impending change that will affect your finances? (i.e. birth of a child, another dependent)

Step 2

Gather any documents needed to support your claims above. This should include income statements, expense records, and recurring or major bills.

If you are interested in additional aid because another college is offering more money, obtain a copy of your award letter from the other school and include it with your supporting documentation. You should also support your appeal with clearly articulated reasons for why a school is your first choice and why you may have to accept the other school's offer because your family cannot afford your first choice with the current aid package offered.

Step 3

How should you contact the financial aid office? If possible, call the office and request an in-person appointment. If that is not possible, you should send a detailed letter via certified mail with documents to support why you believe your aid package should be adjusted. You should make sure to alert a specific financial aid administrator with whom you have already briefly outlined your situation, that a letter will be coming to their attention. Don't just send your letter randomly.

Step 4

Even if your aid package is not adjusted initially, there may be an opportunity months or weeks after your appeal. For example, if you approach a school about work study and they don't have anything available at the time of the appeal, this does not mean they will not have work study later. Or they may be able to steer you towards another on-campus position.

Other Strategies for Shrinking the Tuition Bill

The following information includes a host of strategies you can use to cut your tuition bill.

- Consider certain majors in science, technology, engineering, or mathematics (STEM) related fields. These fields usually have more scholarship money available to them than others.
- If you can do it without completely exhausting yourself, consider completing four years of undergraduate work in three. Or, make sure you finish in four years instead of five or six years.

- Look at institutions that have a matching grant system. In this system if a student who enrolls has an outside scholarship, the institution may match the amount of the outside scholarships up to a certain amount.
- Go to a community college for the first two years. This should cost significantly less than a four-year institution, particularly if you live at home. Using this strategy could potentially get you a degree from an expensive and possibly prestigious institution at a fraction of the cost. If you decide to do this, make sure the courses you take during your first two years will transfer to the four-year school you want to attend and that they will count toward your bachelor's degree.
- Research and look at schools that value your interests. For example, if you are considering an unusual major in which a college or university may be starting a department, you may be able to get a scholarship or reduced tuition from them as they begin looking for students to enroll in their new program.

- If you're looking at the top-tier schools such as Harvard, Yale, or Princeton, consider putting second-tier schools on your prospective list as well. When it comes to financial aid, you may get more assistance from the second-tier schools who accept you.

- Look at universities and colleges where your grades and SAT scores will place you in the top 10 to 25 percent of prospective students. To find this information, consult a guide such as *Peterson's Four-Year Colleges* to find statistics such as these for the freshman class and student body. If your grades and SAT scores are in the top tier of the students the school tries to attract, you have a good chance of securing more aid from the school.

- Consider participating in the AmeriCorps program or a similar program, which allows participants to earn education awards or scholarships in return for some type of service or employment during or after college. For more information about service scholarships, review chapter 14 of *Winning Scholarships for College,*

"Scholarships & Awards for Community Service, Volunteering and Work."

- Consider the military as an option to reduce your costs. The U.S. armed forces offer several educational programs:
  - You can attend one of the military academies. If you are accepted to a military academy you can essentially go to college for four years tuition-free while earning a commission.
  - You can enroll in the Reserve Officers Training Corps (ROTC) program while in college. ROTC will pay for your tuition, fees, and books and may provide you with a monthly allowance.
  - You can join the armed forces before you go to a college and use the Montgomery GI Bill to help pay for college expenses once you've completed your military service.
  - In some instances, you can earn college credit for certain military training. This could possibly

reduce the number of classes
you'll have to take in college.

Scholarships with Late Spring or Summer Deadlines

The following list includes national scholarships with deadlines in mid-April or later of each year. Under no circumstances should this partial list take the place of individual research. Most of the programs are general in nature and should apply to most students nationally. You should make use of the research techniques discussed earlier in this publication to find more scholarships and awards specific to your community and your regional area. You should also do your own research to be certain you have uncovered all opportunities available to you, including new programs that have been implemented since the printing of this publication. Although every effort has been made to ensure the accuracy of the addresses and information listed in this section, some of them may be out of date. If you find an invalid Web address, use an Internet search engine such as Google to find the correct address for the program or scholarship. Or visit www.scholarshipworkshop.com to sign up for our newsletter to get updates and alerts. You can also follow us on Facebook (www.facebook.com/scholarshipworkshop) or on Twitter @ScholarshipWork.

Shawn Carter Foundation
www.shawncartersf.com

Ragins/Braswell National Scholarship
www.scholarshipworkshop.com (see scholarships)

"Stuck at Prom" Contest
www.stuckatprom.com
www.facebook.com/ducktape
twitter.com/theduckbrand

WyzAnt Scholarship Contest
www.wyzant.com/scholarships

Platt Family Scholarship Prize Essay Contest
http://www.thelincolnforum.org/scholarship-essay-contest

Scholarship America Dream Award

Website: www.scholarshipamerica.org or
https://scholarshipamerica.org/dreamaward
Note: You must have completed at least one year of college to apply for this award.

To find additional scholarships, use your favorite search engine and enter the following keywords based on when you are reading this guide:

- Scholarships with *month* deadlines (you select a month to search – for example: scholarships with *March* deadlines)
- Scholarships with spring deadlines
- Scholarships with summer deadlines

APPENDIX

Other Resources from Marianne Ragins

Books and Publications

The Scholarship & College Essay Planning Kit
- If you have trouble getting beyond a blank page when it comes to writing an essay, this resource is for you. This resource is updated yearly.

Get Money for College—An Audio Series
- If you don't have time to read a book or attend a class but you do have time to listen, this audio series can help you learn how to find and win scholarships for college.

10 Steps for Using the Internet in Your Scholarship Search
- This is a resource designed to be used at your computer to walk you step by step through using the Internet for your scholarship search. It keeps you from being overwhelmed by the massive amount of sometimes misleading information found on the web. This resource is updated yearly.

The Scholarship Monthly Planning Calendar
- This convenient and easy to use monthly planning calendar will help you with time

management, getting organized, and staying on track with activities to meet major scholarship and award deadlines. This resource is updated yearly.

Winning Scholarships for College
- In *Winning Scholarships for College*, Marianne Ragins, the winner of more than $400,000 in scholarship funds, proves that it`s not always the students with the best grades or the highest SAT scores who win scholarships. Whether you are in high school, returning to or currently enrolled in college, or planning to study abroad, this easy to follow college scholarship guide will show you the path to scholarship success. One of the most comprehensive books on winning scholarships and written by a successful scholarship recipient, it reveals where and how to search for funds, and walks you step by step through the scholarship application process.

Last Minute College Financing Guide
- If you've got the acceptance letter, but are still wondering how to pay the tuition bill because you haven't yet started searching for college money, this resource is for you!

Workshops & Boot Camps

The Scholarship Workshop Presentation

- In The Scholarship Workshop presentation, which is a 1, 2, or 3 hour interactive seminar, speaker Marianne Ragins, proves that it is not always the student with the best grades or the highest SAT scores who wins scholarships. Instead she shows students of all ages that most scholarships are awarded to students who exhibit the best preparation. By attending The Scholarship Workshop presentation, a student will be well prepared to meet the challenge of finding and winning scholarships. The presentation is designed to help students conduct a successful scholarship search from the research involved in finding scholarship money to the scholarship essays, scholarship interview tips and strategies involved in winning them. This presentation is usually sponsored by various organizations and individuals usually attend at no cost. Attendees of the presentation become eligible for the Ragins/Braswell National scholarship sponsored by Marianne. If you or your organization is interested in sponsoring a workshop or motivational presentation with Marianne Ragins, visit www.scholarshipworkshop.com.

The Scholarship Workshop Boot Camp

- This is an expanded version of The Scholarship Workshop presentation—It is a full day and a half of activities designed to help students and parents leave the weekend with scholarship essays, résumés, and applications completed and ready to go. The workshop boot camp is usually sponsored by various organizations and individuals usually attend at no cost. Attendees of the presentation become eligible for the Ragins/Braswell National scholarship sponsored by Marianne. If you or your organization is interested in sponsoring a workshop or motivational presentation with Marianne Ragins, visit www.scholarshipworkshop.com.

Webinars & Online Classes

- *The Scholarship Class for High School Students and Their Parents*
- *Scholarship, Fellowship & Grant Information Session for Students Already in College, Returning to College, and Pursuing Graduate School*
    - o The above classes are webinar versions of the Scholarship Workshop presentation. It is offered for those who do not live in an area where a workshop is being

sponsored. Attendees of either class become eligible for the Ragins/Braswell National Scholarship.

- *Writing Scholarship & College Essays for the Uneasy Student Writer* — A Webinar
- *Turbocharge Your Résumé - Résumé Writing Skills to Help You Stand Out from the Crowd* — A Webinar
- *Preparation Skills for Scholarship & College Interviews* — A Webinar
- *Minimizing College Costs and Student Loans* — A Webinar

For more information about webinars and online classes available, visit www.scholarshipworkshop.com (see online classes)

eBooks

Marianne Ragins also has numerous e-Books available for Nook, Kindle and iPad. Visit www.scholarshipworkshop.com (see eBooks) for the latest!

You can find information and additional resources from Marianne Ragins by visiting or connecting with her using the following:

- www.scholarshipworkshop.com
- www.facebook.com/scholarshipworkshop
- www.twitter.com/ScholarshipWork
- www.scholarshipworkshop.com/bookstore

ABOUT THE AUTHOR

In her senior year of high school, Marianne Ragins won over $400,000 in scholarships for college. As perhaps the first student ever to amass nearly half a million dollars in scholarship money, she has been featured in many publications including *USA Today, People, Ebony, Newsweek, Money, Essence, Family Money, Black Enterprise* and on the cover of *Parade*. She has also made hundreds of radio and television appearances on shows such as "Good Morning America," "The Home Show," and the "Mike & Maty Show."

Marianne Ragins received a master of business administration (MBA) from George Washington University in Washington, DC and a bachelor of science (BS) degree in business administration from Florida Agricultural and Mechanical University in Tallahassee, Florida. Both degrees were entirely funded by scholarships and other free aid.

Marianne Ragins is also the author of the highly successful *Winning Scholarships for College: An Insider's Guide* and many other publications. She is an experienced motivational speaker and lecturer who has traveled nationally and internationally conducting The Scholarship Workshop presentation and giving other motivational seminars and speeches. Marianne is the publisher of www.scholarshipworkshop.com, a scholarship and college information site, and sponsor of the *Leading the Future II* and *Ragins Braswell National Scholarships*.

Contact Marianne Ragins using any of the following sources:
- www.scholarshipworkshop.com
- www.facebook.com/scholarshipworkshop
- www.twitter.com/ScholarshipWork